Winter Nature Activities for

Irmgard Kutsch and Brigitte Walden

Winter Nature Activities for Children

Rudolf Steiner College Press

Translated by Jane R. Helmchen

First published in German in 2001 as
Natur-Kinder-Garten-Werkstatt: Winter,
by Verlag Freies Geistesleben, Stuttgart
First published in English in 2006
by Rudolf Steiner College Press, California,
and Floris Books, Edinburgh
Second printing 2011

Publication of this book has been made possible by a grant
from the Waldorf Curriculum Fund

ISBN 978-086315-564-2
Printed in China

February (Part 2)

*A good snowfall always encourages
fun and enthusiastic play*

Foreword

Teaching children about the environment could be seen as something of a survival strategy for the modern world. Children need an awareness and an understanding of nature in order that they might care for it and sustain it for the future. Awareness of environmental issues has increased; however, still too few people act in an ecologically responsible way.

In the 1970s the environmental lobby adopted a 'catastrophe' approach: warning the world of impending environmental doom, be it air or water pollution, or dying forests, unless action was taken. Unfortunately this led not to action, but to resignation: people felt helpless and therefore indifferent. Today, we know that a positive relationship with nature is a much better base for preservation and protection.

If you ask people involved today in environmental protection about their childhood memories, they often talk about living in or visiting the country, or about their own small vegetable patch, walks in the woods with their parents, building huts or playing in puddles. They experienced the wonders of nature as children: the magic of a butterfly slipping out of its cocoon, or the beauty of a wild-flower meadow. As children, they enjoyed watching a bird feeding its young, the fragrance of a herb garden, the delicacy of freshly picked strawberries, or the fragrance of freshly hulled peas.

We know that childhood experiences are formative and hugely significant. Regular encounters with the natural world are central to the healthy development of a growing child. What can we expect from people growing up in a time of increasingly frantic technology, stress, consumerism and continual stimulation through television and the computer? Such constant irritation dulls the senses, and limits a child's movement. In addition, it can cause disturbances in a child's sense of self and connection with the world, leading to well-known symptoms such as hyperactivity, posture problems, nervousness, an inability to concentrate, and even learning disabilities. This can hardly be seen as a good basis for being responsible with nature. And yet the generations to come will need even more nature protectors.

Young children need adults to help and guide them in their understanding of nature

Opposites: on a cold, wintry evening, hot wax candles with a summer fragrance are very popular

When, some time ago, Irmgard Kutsch told me about her ideas for this series of books, I was immediately enthusiastic and convinced that the books would lead to a gentle caring for nature. The books consider the needs of children and their changing world. They promote holistic encounters with nature in an interesting and lively manner, and demonstrate ways in which children can understand nature and its seasons with all of their senses, through practical work.

Experiencing nature is not limited to a few months of the year. The Nature Activities for Children series offers countless suggestions for discoveries and experiences in all four seasons which will engage the feelings and train the senses. Children become involved with the rhythm of the year, and feel more grounded. They follow processes through from start to finish: rather than beginning with beeswax, they start with the beehive, so they know how the wax is produced. They learn about seeds of grain and follow the path from grain to bread — and enjoy tasting their own delicious home-baked loaf. This contrasts strongly with our society where work is divided into small, individual steps, and each of us actually produces very little.

Irmgard Kutsch approaches these books with determination, love and understanding, just as she approaches the running of the Children's Nature and Garden Centre. She firmly believes that we learn best by doing.

This *Winter* volume focuses on traditional handicraft techniques, using materials drawn from nature: wood, wool, clay. By working with natural materials — dyeing wool, weaving, making baskets or pressing juice — children learn that keeping traditional processes alive is a way to help preserve nature.

Although there is a good deal of literature on this subject, I admire this particular contribution because it brings together many disciplines, uses nature-based approaches, and comes entirely from the practical experience of the authors. Because of this, the instructions are especially vivid, convincing and easy to put into practice.

This series of book offers projects that children are unlikely to find anywhere else. It is a valuable resource for teaching about nature, and is therefore an important contribution to nature preservation itself. These books will certainly not gather dust on a bookshelf.

I hope that Irmgard Kutsch and Brigitte Walden will reach many teachers and parents and that their books will encourage increasing involvement with nature so that as many children as possible can grow in a healthy environment, and can experience the continuing wonder of nature. This is what will sow the seed for a life of responsibility for nature.

Dagmar Israel, Northern Region Director of the German Environment Aid Association

The Story of this Book

Making room for play

In winter, as in every season, lots of children come to the Children's Nature and Garden Centre. They find out what's new in nature and start playing very quickly, and with great imagination. They might test the ice on the birdbaths or water barrels, or build detailed snowmen. They make long, narrow tobaggan runs, with especially difficult bits to test their skill, strength and courage. Through games like this, they bond with one another and form communities.

Afterwards, soaked through, exhausted and cold, all they want is dry clothes, food and warmth.

Learning about opposites

During the winter months at the Centre there are both quiet activities, such as making candles or working with wax, and more active projects, such as creating Christmas scenes, making raw wool into yarn and rugs, carving wooden toys, and making pottery. Winter is a season of opposites, and children thrive on the contrast created by opposites.

Moving from outdoors to indoors demonstrates the opposites of cold and warmth, darkness and light, and night and day. Feeling wet and feeling dry, or feeling hungry and feeling full, also work as powerful opposites for children. In the winter, the opposites of movement and stillness come together: frost calls for active energy; coldness can be overcome by a warming fire.

Children can therefore learn, through play, to recognise opposites as stimulants for action.

Today's children will make tomorrow's decisions for the world and we should encourage a willingness to act and to be innovative, to solve the problems inherited from previous generations. We also need to encourage cross-cultural communication — easier now with modern technology — and cross-generational cooperation.

The start of these responsibilities can be seen in many of the hands-on nature activities that we do at the Centre. It goes without saying that we encourage children of all backgrounds and religions to join in with the Centre's programmes; all we ask is a respect for human rights and a willingness to work with those who are different from us.

The Children's Nature and Garden Centre

The idea behind the Children's Nature and Garden Centre is to encourage the development, and deepening, of values from our cultural history which can point the way for the future. We try to be positive role-models to the children at the Centre, in how we think, feel and act. In this way, they can gain a holistic view of the world, learn to respect nature and be a force for peace in the world.

This series of books, therefore, has been written for the adults who want to accompany children on their path of nature discovery.

Irmgard Kutsch

December

Advent

Winter has arrived. The first snowfall draws children outside, and soon there are lots of snowmen, or in some cases, snow-animals. It's wonderful to see how individual each snow sculpture is, lovingly crafted by small hands.

Sadly, some of these exotic creatures may soon find themselves on the list of endangered species. For one thing, climate change could mean an increase in temperature in many areas, with fewer opportunities to play in the snow. In addition, many children don't seem to know instinctively *how* to play in the snow; this is something which can be easily overcome by parents and teachers leading the way and encouraging and demonstrating creative ideas.

At the time when the sun reaches its lowest position on December 21, the day of the winter solstice under the zodiac sign of Sagittarius (♐), the plant world is dormant, waiting for a new cycle of life. The ground is bare. Protected underground, seeds lie in quiet expectation. And yet the upward-pointing arrow in the symbol for Sagittarius represents the awakening of nature at the winter solstice: the earth has only seemed quiet, but in fact plants will soon be stirring into life, pushing upwards towards the surface. It is a slow, tranquil process, as symbolized by the horizontal line on the Sagittarius symbol.

Hedgehogs, hamsters and bats have long since been in hibernation, and squirrels only interrupt their winter sleep to nibble on their cache of collected food. Moles dig through the frozen ground, creating fresh piles of earth in the snow. Snakes and frogs grow rigid as they sink gradually into hibernation, and snails close up their shell entrances. Some types of butterfly hang lifelessly in protected places and wait for the spring.

Pets need particular attention at this time of year. In the winter, they are totally dependent on caring human beings. This has never been so important as it is today, when disregard for life has reached staggering proportions.

The North Wind Does Blow

1 The north wind does blow＿ and we shall have snow, and what will the rob - in do then, poor thing? He'll
2 The north wind does blow＿ and we shall have snow, and what will the swal - low do then, poor thing? Oh,

sit in the barn and keep him - self warm, and hide his head un - der his wing, poor thing.
do you not know he's gone long a - go to a coun - try much warm - er than ours, poor thing.

The seed-bearing plants in the herb spiral (see the Spring *book for instructions) are a winter food source for birds*

Advent: a Time for Contemplation

Winter is a good time for getting a different perspective on everyday outdoor objects. See how different the garden looks with snow piled on the fence posts, with the last berries on the bushes wearing little snow caps, and with benches or the sandbox buried and white. It's also interesting to notice how many variations of whiteness there are in the snow: it can be a cold red in the morning, blinding in the glistening midday sun, and have a blue shimmer at dusk. Our own shadows, or those of trees, can seem to stretch on endlessly in the low sunlight.

Now is the time of Advent, a period of contemplation and expectation. The darkness becomes deeper, and the outer world colder. In our part of the world, people begin to prepare for Christmas.

A child's drawing of the winter solstice reveals an inner connection to cosmic events

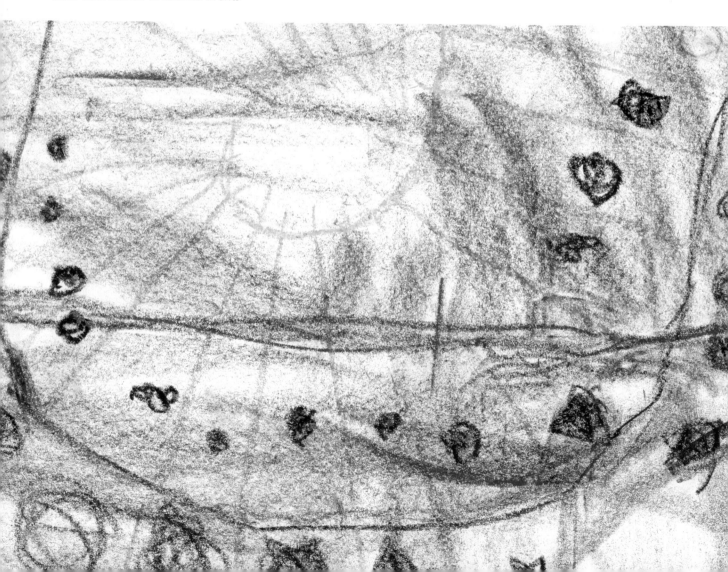

Advent

Now the twilight of the year
Comes, and Christmas draws near.
See, across the Advent sky
How the clouds move quietly.
Earth is waiting, wrapped in sleep,
Waiting in a silence deep.
Birds are hid in bush and reed
Flowers are sleeping in their seed.

Through the woodland to and fro
Silent-footed creatures go.
Hedgehog curled in prickly ball
Burrows 'neath the leaves that fall.
Man and beast and bird and flower
Waiting for the midnight hour
Waiting for the Christ-child's birth
Christ who made the heaven and earth.

Ann Ellerton

The ideas and values of Christmas can be renewed and revived when working with children in December. This is especially important when traditions are dying out, and consumerism is taking an ever-tighter hold on our festive holidays. We should encourage an inner quiet and contemplation of the coming of the light — not a natural state for children perhaps, but one which must be consciously adopted each year anew. From the huge range of Advent customs and traditions on offer, we have selected, for this book, those that symbolize hope and expectation, and point towards things other than themselves.

An enchanted world: the round benches of the willow hut covered in white (see the Spring *book for instructions on building a willow arbour)*

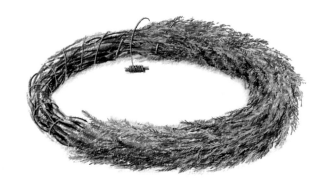

The Advent Wreath

Children like to help make the Advent wreath, and the whole room fills with the fragrance of the pine branches.

Use branches from trees that don't drop their needles as much (for example, Douglas fir, Nordman fir or the common pine). You can also add other evergreens, such as boxwood, cherry laurel and ivy, into the wreath.

Cut off lengths of about 8 inches (20 cm). Overlap the larger branches, binding them with wire as you go to form a stable ring as the base of the wreath. Then place the finer branches onto the base in layers, and secure with wire.

This pre-Christmas period is filled with secrets, surprises and little gifts. Children love to discover the fragrant green Advent wreath decorated for the first Advent Sunday, if possible with four handsome beeswax candles. This, and experiencing the growing light from the candles as Christmas nears, will form some of their most vivid childhood memories.

This poem can accompany the lighting of the Advent wreath:

Around the Advent Wreath

The gift of light I thankfully hold
And pass to my neighbour, its shining gold
That everyone may feel its glow,
Receiving and giving, may love and grow.

When everyone has lit a light
No more shall continue the darkness of night.
A joyful message we shall hear:
"Look and see, the Christ draws near!"

Traditional

Advent: a Time for Candles

Making candles, pouring the wax, and dyeing and decorating candles are especially symbolic activites for this time of year. Warm, light candles burning in the cold darkness represent an inner light that we should encourage during Advent season. Candles also make great presents; the *Autumn* book in this series includes instructions on dipping beeswax candles.

Ideally, children should understand where beeswax comes from, but it's normally only possible to see bees in action during the warmer seasons (see the *Spring* book in this series for more information).

Blowing Ships

Use a water container, such as a portable sandbox or a clean basin, as the base for a natural landscape. Place odd-shaped roots, pretty stones, moss-covered bark, twigs and so on into the container, which, when the container is filled with water, will create shipping lanes and ports. Attach small candles into walnut shells. The game is to blow the tiny candle ships through the shipping lanes from the port of departure to the port of arrival, without blowing out the candle flame.

For blowing ships well, the breath of air must be controlled and well-directed. Children should be at least six years old

White candles can be dipped into coloured liquid wax for decoration. The working area is protected with a burlap cloth.

Children make candle-holders out of clay, decorate them with beechnut shells, and then insert the candles

An Advent Story

Far away in the East there lived a very good man called Bishop Nicholas. One day, he was told that there was a city far away in the West where everyone was starving, even the children. He called together all his loving servants and said, "Bring me the food from your gardens and your fields so that we can stop the children in the city from starving."

The servants brought apples and nuts in baskets, and on top they placed honey cakes. Others brought wheat grain in sacks. Bishop Nicholas had all the food loaded onto a ship with white and blue sails, as white as the clouds and as blue as Bishop Nicholas's coat.

The wind blew the sails and the ship moved quickly over the water. When the wind was tired, the sailors pulled at the oars and rowed the ship to the city far away in the West. They travelled a long way, for seven days and seven nights.

When they arrived at the big city, it was evening. There was no one in the streets, but lights burned in the windows of the houses. Bishop Nicholas knocked at a window. The mother in the house thought it was a late wanderer, and her child opened the door. But there was no one there. The child ran to the window, but there was no one there either.

But a basket was there, filled with apples and nuts and honey cake. Next to the basket was a sack with golden wheat grains spilling out. Baskets with apples, nuts and honey cake and sacks with wheat grains stood in front of the doors of the other houses too. All the people in the city ate the presents and became healthy and happy again.

Today, St Nicholas is in heaven. However, every year on his birthday he makes a trip back to earth. He orders his white horse and rides from star to star, bringing gifts to children. Where Nicholas cannot go himself, he lends his voice to good people and asks them to deliver, in his name, apples, nuts and honey cake.

Blooming Branches

Around the start of December (in Germany, this is done on St Barbara's Day on December 4), cut branches from a cherry, apple, plum or almond tree, or from a forsythia bush, winter jasmine or horse chestnut. Place them overnight in lukewarm water then put them in a jug of water in a moderately warm room. Change the water every three days, and trim the branches from time to time. The branches will bloom on Christmas Day, making a wonderful display that the children will remember.

Rattling Walnuts

For each child, split a walnut into two perfect halves, hollow it out, paint it gold and fill it with wheat grains, which have been saved as seeds for the coming spring. Place a loop of thread between the walnut halves and glue them back together. When the children shake the nuts, they'll hear a mysterious rattling. In German-speaking cultures, this is part of the celebration of St Nicholas Day on December 6: St Nicholas tells the children that it's a secret why the nut rattles, and that the secret will last until Easter when they can open the nuts. Children can take the nuts home and hang them on the Christmas tree.

The rattling walnuts represent the symbolic winter rest of the grain until the next growing season. It's important for a teacher or parent to present the rattling walnuts as a mysterious thing; a scientific explanation would only dispel the magic. If you think that the magic might not survive the trip home, the nuts can be used to decorate a branch in the classroom, until spring arrives.

Christmas Scenes

Christmas is a good time to look back on everything that has happened in the past year. The most beautiful, successful and valuable objects from the children's nature activites throughout the previous twelve months can be collected together to make a joyous Christmas or Nativity scene.

Every morning during Advent, children can find something which can be added to the Christmas scene. For the first week they could collect objects from the mineral kingdom, followed in

Roots can be collected to form the background and living structure of a Christmas scene. The children can remove bits of earth and loose material to reveal the intricate detail of the roots; this is best done using a wire brush or an old toothbrush.

Some children like working with wire brushes; others prefer a mallet, chisel, knife or saw

Some roots might fall victim to over-energetic hands, but adults should put aside their aesthetic sensitivies in favour of the child's enthusiasm

subsequent weeks by things from the plant and animal kingdoms.

If you're able to plan a year's worth of activities leading up to the making of a Christmas scene, you might find this schedule useful:

* In January, create human and animal figures out of wool. They appear in the Christmas scene as Mary with the child, as Joseph, as the shepherds and as the kings.
* In February, build the stable from round sticks. It will offer protection for people and animals. Candleholders and vases can also be made from clay.

- In March, sow the grain from the rattling walnuts (see page 19). You can use straw to make stars for the dark pine branches.
- In April, designate the area in the garden where the poinsettia will grow.
- In May, use natural plant dyes to dye the cloth for the base and backdrop.
- In June, fill a pot-pourri bag with rose petals and save the nicest butterfly cocoons.
- In July, when you're on country walks, collect beautiful objects from the mineral, plant and animal worlds.
- In August, harvest the straw for Baby Jesus' cradle.
- In September, choose a few fragrant winter apples from the tree.
- In October, weave a small cradle basket for Baby Jesus or build a simple hut from natural materials to serve as the stable.
- In November, make the beeswax candles to light the Christmas scene.
- In December, an entire yearly cycle, in which the children have been actively involved, comes to an end before their very eyes.

A Christmas scene, such as an artistic Advent calendar filled with handicrafts, can present an overview of yearly themes in nature — an ideal way for a child to understand the end of a calendar year

An important goal of the Children's Nature and Garden Centre is to create a social community through craft and activity projects. To build a Christmas scene, for example, people have to listen to each other and learn from each other; and in doing so, they experience the real meaning of the Christmas season. For generations, our ancestors experienced Christmas in a different way: they lived in real darkness at this time of year, which made the night-time stars even brighter, giving them greater hope. The frost on the window panes glistened, and made people feel connected to the elements. They made a special effort to clean their houses for the festive season.

Today, the natural darkness is driven out by a flood of artificial light. Double-glazed windows prevent frost and our hygienic culture and easy-care cleaning products make special preparations unnecessary. Some of the once-a-year magic of Advent has been lost.

The figures of the Christmas scene shown here were made from beeswax mixed with lanolin (see the Autumn book in this series for instructions)

Coloured beeswax can also be used to make Christmas scene figures. The base of this scene is a slice of tree trunk and the covering has been woven out of jute twine.

Parents build a Christmas scene for a kindergarten classroom. During autumn, plants were hung up to dry in preparation. The figures are made of clay.
➤

The True Meaning of Advent

To understand Advent you have to take a long journey into the past, to the prophets of Israel whose message has been given to us in the Old Testament. Their great theme is God's sense of justice for the weak and powerless, and his loyalty to us human beings in spite of our sins. They speak of a future in which God will give people a new beginning, in which he creates peace and healing, and which will influence everything including nature. Furthermore, God will come out of concealment and will create a close relationship between himself and human beings. This arrival of God at the end of time is the theme of the Advent season. During Advent there is great hope for all humankind and for all creation. The story does not end in chaos or the collapse of the world, but rather in the rise of the world. The Bible also calls this future the "Kingdom of God".

During Advent, we not only look forward to the future that God holds for us, but we also look back and think about the coming of Jesus Christ. In Jesus of Nazareth, God came into our world to be close to all those who are suffering, who are oppressed or are without hope, to share in their lives. Christmas,

◄ *Every year, a biodynamic farm performs the Christmas story in its natural setting, for an audience of several hundred people*

the miracle of God becoming human, is the guarantee of our great hope for the world.

But misery, injustice and suffering have not yet been conquered. People are still violent toward one another and commit crimes against God's creation instead of protecting it.

For this reason, Christians remember during Advent that Jesus Christ, crucified and risen from the dead, will come again to fulfil all the prophecies of the prophets of Israel and finally to manifest God's loyalty to this world.

Just as children can only ask about the stars when they have looked at them from their earthly perspective, interest and curiosity about other cultures and religions can only develop after people have found their own foundation in their own culture. During Advent, many opportunities for questions and discussion arise; for example, during a kindergarten Christmas celebration, a discussion about the festivities of other religions can enrich the atmosphere for all the children present.

Reverend Wolfgang Vorländer

Children sorting semi-precious stones on a board with indentations, according to colours, sizes or shapes. In winter this is a particularly popular way of handling natural materials. When the Christmas scene is taking shape, the coloured stones can decorate Mary and Joseph's path to the stable. ▼

Other Religious Festivals

In addition to the many books available on various cultural and religious traditions, a great deal of information can be found easily on the internet.

✿ *Eid ul Fitr* ("Festival of Breaking") is the Islamic festival of breaking the fast of the holy month of Ramadan. The focus is on breaking bad habits. There are prayers in large gatherings thanking the Creator for all blessings, followed by visits to the homes of friends and relatives.
    www.crescentlife.com/spirituality

✿ *Diwali* ("A Row of Lamps") is a Hindu festival in which thousands of lamps are lit in the dark time of the year. Firecrackers are set off at the beginning of the celebration and houses are decorated to welcome home the divine King Rama and Queen Sita after their 14 years of exile.
    www.diwalifestival.org

✿ *Hanukkah* ("Dedication") is the Jewish festival of lights lasting eight days and nights. It celebrates the rededication of the Temple in Jerusalem after the Hebrew people were freed from the Syrian Empire by Judah Maccabee.
    www.jewfaq.org/holiday

✿ *Kwanzaa* ("First") is an African-American cultural festival held from December 26 to January 1. It was founded in 1966 by Dr Maulana Karenga to celebrate the traditional African values of family, community responsibility, commerce and self-improvement. (It is not a substitute for Christmas.)
    www.tike.com

Further information

Buddhist celebration of the new year:
    www.buddhanet/ceremony
Native American customs:
    www.ganondagan.org/winter-festival
Jain, Shinto, Sikh, Taoist and Zoroastrian customs:
    www.wheeloftheyear.com

January

Working with Wool

When you walk around outside in January, the earth's surface seems dead and bare. The air is frosty and cold; the ground is frozen. At times, white snow covers the countryside.

The animals that live outdoors and do not hibernate now need continual care. This is especially true of the birds that stay here over the winter. We describe their special care in the *Autumn* book in this series. It is especially important that a snow- and ice-free birdbath be available in a frost-resistant vessel. When ponds and streams are frozen, water is even more important than seeds and fat.

January stands mainly under the zodiac sign of Capricorn (♑), the Wild Goat, which influences new growth in plants: under the earth, seeds are being encouraged to come to life. The wild goat stands alone on mountainous cliffs, and looks around as if searching for new challenges that will provide its strength and agility. It defends its area with a dark expression and a thrust of its powerful horns. Even young goats show these characteristics, by kicking and leaping.

The character of the wild goat reflects what is happening in the earth at this time of year: activity is starting, and seed hulls are beginning to open up. This is necessary so that, during the next zodiac sign of Aquarius (♒), the Water Bearer, life-bringing water can be absorbed by the germinating seeds.

In January, the length of the days increases by almost one hour. At the same time, children become more interested in activities. But children cannot play in snow and ice all the time; outdoor play time is often very limited because of cold or wet weather. Children need an interesting, active project with warm material in warm surroundings. January is therefore a good time to introduce children to working with wool.

Working with Wool: a Rich Experience

The production of yarn and cloth has played a central role in human history. It's hard to imag-

ine life without textiles made into clothes, both today and for the future. It's therefore not only out of nostalgia that we should introduce children to working with wool. Learning to card, spin, weave, crochet and knit are all excellent experiences.

For one thing, they learn traditional craft skills, and if the activities are accompanied by appropriate songs, games, poems and stories, children gain a greater understanding of how these skills form part of their cultural history.

When this farm child, not yet two years old, saw the white garden for the very first time, the amazed reaction was "Oh, milk!" She was even more surprised to explore this wintry secret by looking at, feeling and tasting — snow.

Processing Wool

Since ancient times, people have used the wool, hair and fur of animals to protect themselves from cold and wet weather. Sheep's wool has been especially important, because it has particular characteristics such as the ability to take in and give off moisture and warmth. Wool is therefore able to keep our body at a comfortable temperature.

Wool hairs have scales like those of a pine cone. Wool grease, called lanolin, is found in the scales; this keeps the wool hairs soft. When processing the wool, however, the lanolin gums up the fine teeth of the machine, so it must be washed out. This is done with chemical soap. After the lanolin is removed, the wool is brittle and can become static. In order to make the wool soft again, chemical oil is added. The chemist must always ensure that the soap and oil used will not be detrimental to human health.

Wool grows in a variety of ways. There are long, short, thick, thin, crimped, colourful and brittle wools. In order to spin a good thread, several types of wool must be mixed together, and for this, a mixing table is used. The individual wools are layered on top of each other and are

put into a machine with rotating drums that have coarse teeth. Because of these big teeth, the machine is known as "the wolf". The wolf tears apart the clumps of wool so that the individual fibres can be laid free.

The next machine is the wool carder. It is built like the wolf but has only very fine teeth. These teeth pull the fibres of the wool until they are parallel to each other. The fibres are then separated into narrow bands and move on to the spinning machine. The finished yarn can now be knitted, crocheted or woven.

There is not enough wool to meet the demand for clothes, so alternatives — synthetic fibres — were developed. Synthetic fibres are made from a solution that is pressed through nozzles with fine openings. The diameter of the openings determines the thickness of the fibres. After going through the nozzles, the fibres are fixed by a chemical bath so that they don't stick to each other, and they're cut to the desired length. Here, too, the chemist must be careful to use only substances that do not damage human health.

Adolf Gast (in front) at his giant wool carder. Children who have tried to card wool by hand can understand what this machine does.

Adolf Gast, a spinning master who cares for old spinning machines and looms in a museum

30

Clothing: Our Second Skin

Anyone who has tried to make yarn on a spinning machine with coordinated treading and turning movements, and has seen how a strong, tight thread emerges, has developed a sure feel for the quality of yarn and cloth. Even a preschool child can understand that we choose our clothes to give us a shell of air and warmth, and to protect us from rain or too much sun.

Clothing is, so to speak, our second skin, with which we human beings adapt to the conditions of nature.

In this age of allergies, the quality of clothing and its dyes cannot be underestimated. When children who are dressed head-to-toe in synthetic fibres, for example, move about a bit, heat builds up under their clothes. Body moisture cannot escape; the children end up drenched in sweat and can get chilled by the slightest cold breeze.

On the other hand, clothing made from wool can, due to the open nature and elasticity of the fibres, trap large amounts of air and thereby insulate the body. Wool can also absorb up to forty percent of its own weight in moisture, without feeling damp, which means sweat doesn't build up on the skin. Germs and bacteria don't settle on wool, because of the scales on the individual wool hairs. The lanolin in wool also has a healing effect: lanolin is an important base for ointments. Sheared wool is therefore perfect for maintaining a comfortable body temperature. It protects us equally well from cold, moisture and heat.

Children who have learned to take good care of themselves and their health will often, as adults, be more sensitive towards how we treat the earth and the atmosphere. They're more likely to adopt attitudes towards consumerism and materialism which question their effect on nature and the environment.

For example, they might question how the raw material for a piece of clothing was produced: did its creation involve pesticides, synthetic fertilizers, delousing agents, poisonous bleaches, softeners or chemical dyes, which could affect the material, the human workers or the environment? Was all the processing done in one location, to save on transportation energy? What were the

Working with wool in a kindergarten

working conditions like for the people who made it? Companies manufacturing clothes should be prepared to make full declarations about the origin of their products.

Those who have hands-on experience of working with wool and yarn are in a much better position to appreciate what might go on behind a factory wall. In addition, an understanding of production technology can be beneficial to other aspects of life. The more children can learn and understand today, the better prepared they'll be to address and manage their social and ecological responsibilities tomorrow.

Children can often grasp the basic mechanical principles in a wool workshop ▼

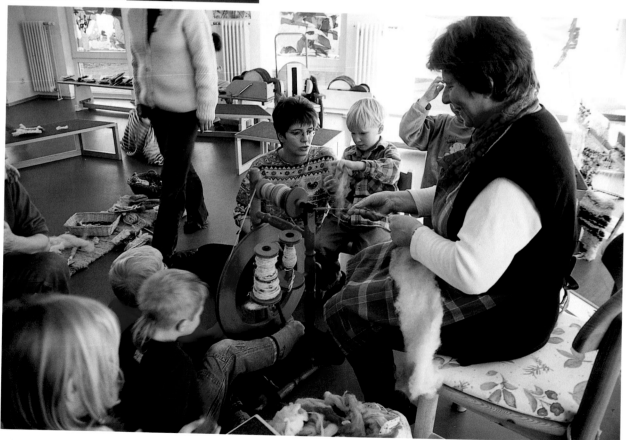

◄ *Shearing the sheep carefully and skilfully, with a firm grip*

Wool: from the Sheep to a Ball of Wool

Children normally participate in wool workshops with great enthusiasm. There are lots of hands-on activities suitable for children of different ages. The process of obtaining and then working with wool, from the sheep to a ball of wool which can become a woven rug or knitted sweater, is long and full of hard work. Adults must lead by example in this area.

⌐ Shearing sheep

Human attitudes towards animals and their treatment are gradually improving. An especially interesting development is the movement in different countries to protect threatened domestic species, such as particular breeds of cows, horses, pigs, poultry, goats, rabbits and sheep. Some specialist farms are implementing breeding programmes to restore stocks; a visit to such a farm is a wonderful educational experience for children. (See the Resources section in the back of this book for the contact details of organisations working in this field.)

A visit to a shepherd is also an impressive experience for children and adults alike, especially if you get a chance to see sheep shearing in action. The waterproof fur coat of a sheep

◄ *Outdoor festivals and agricultural fairs are good places for children to experience sheep shearing*

33

▲ *Washing wool with old beaters: a favourite activity at the Children's Nature and Garden Centre*

⌐ Cleaning and drying the wool

The wool must next be cleaned of all loose dirt. To do this, soak the wool for several hours in a barrel filled with rain water. During this time, it must be stirred and beaten a few times, either with old beaters as in the picture to the left, or with bare feet. Hang it up to dry, then carefully pull it apart to release the bits of dirt. Repeat the whole procedure until the wool is nice and clean. Ideally, this task should be done outdoors; the best time is in the summer after the sheep have been sheared.

⌐ Carding

The first step in processing the cleaned wool is carding, which loosens up the wool. It can be done without any equipment: simply pull the wool apart with your fingers to make a fine veil. It can be described to children as making the wool thin enough so that light can shine through, or

contains an enormous amount of wool, and its high lanolin content prevents rain from reaching the animal's skin.

Tin tubs are good for washing wool outdoors; wash the wool in rainwater or well-water if possible, but remember not to use detergent so as not to remove the lanolin ➤

34

◄ *Wool can be dried on anything from laundry racks and compost sieves to ladders covered with fishing nets. Sun and wind make the wool light and fluffy; the wool can then be pulled apart by hand, letting any loose dirt fall out.*

as delicate as a butterfly's wings, or as fine as a snowflake.

Older children can try using hand carders, between which the wool is brushed. The most dexterous children might like to try a carding drum. You need to be careful not to put too much wool between the large and small brushing cylinders. This technique needs a lot of patience to produce a nice thick wool fleece.

◄ *Only small pre-worked sections of wool which can be easily gripped should be used in the carding machine, to prevent it from becoming blocked*

Children are often keen to try out the carding drum ▼

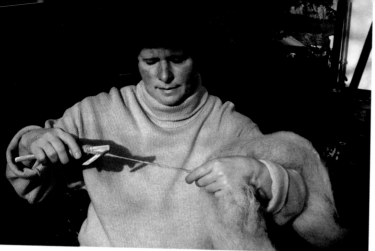

Spinning wool with a branch hook spindle

~ Spinning

The next step is to spin the wool, and a stick spindle can be used easily to make the carefully carded wool into thread.

To make a stick spindle, take a stick that is 6–8 inches (15–20 cm) long and about ¹/₂ inch (1 cm) thick, cut off the bark and sand it smooth.

To spin using a stick spindle, two children must sit opposite each other. One child holds a handful of carded wool, while the other carefully pulls out wool fibres, twists them into a thread in a clockwise direction, and wraps the thread around the stick spindle. Pulling, turning and wrapping should be done rhymically.

Another simple way of spinning is with a branch hook spindle. The branch hook is turned on its long axis with one hand, while the other hand holds the carded wool. This is a good way of spinning very fine, very strong yarn. Even six year olds can spin using a branch hook if they've developed enough feeling for the wool beforehand.

Carving and sanding the stick spindle

Working with a drop spindle is too difficult for children, but it is still worth demonstrating this age-old tool used in many cultures. While the

Spinning thread with a partner is a very good way of learning cooperation

Spinning with a drop spindle

Spinning, then, is a symbolic human activity, and one in which children invariably participate enthusiastically. They let their wool bundles be pulled into the spinning wheel and watch how the fibres are twisted together in a spiral, and wound around the bobbin. The spinning process is especially transparent if you use wool of different colours. And remember, regardless of the tool, spinning is always done in a clockwise direction.

It can be easier for children to learn rhymical skills such as spinning if appropriate songs or rhymes accompany the activity. One five year old sensed the connection between singing and working: he refused to start spinning until the right song was sung. He was convinced that the spinning wheel would only start to turn once the children were singing.

Over the page is a traditional American song that imitates the sounds of the quickly spinning wheel.

adult forms the thread, the children have great fun keeping the spindle rotating fast enough. As soon as the thread has the right twist, it is wound around the rotating disc or block.

Children are often fascinated by a moving spinning wheel, and want to know how it works. From a pile of jumbled wool, a strong thread develops and is wound round a bobbin. Watching wool being spun acts as a good metaphor for a logical train of thought: the phrases "losing the thread" and "picking up the thread again" take on new meaning.

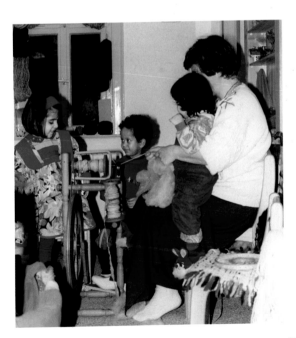

Children are often fascinated by traditional skills such as spinning yarn, and impatiently wait their turn ➤

Sarasponda

Drone during verse

Boom - da, boom-da, boom-da, boom-da.

Verse

Sa - ra - spon - da, Sa - ra - spon - da, Sa - ra - spon - da, Ret - set - set! Sa - ra -

spon - da, Sa - ra - spon - da, Sa - ra - spon - da, Ret - set - set!

Refrain (all together)

Ah - do - day - oh! Ah - do - ray - boom - day - oh! Ah -

do - ray - boom - day - ret - set - set! Ah - say - pah - say - oh!

Twisting

When two bobbins are full, the two threads can be twisted together to make a stronger thread. To do this, a new bobbin — onto which the double thread is to be wound — is turned in a counter-clockwise direction.

If spun yarn is used as a single ply, or untwisted, thread, the cloth made from it can be easily pulled out of shape, especially after being washed several times. This can be seen, for example, in cotton

Twisting threads with a stone weight

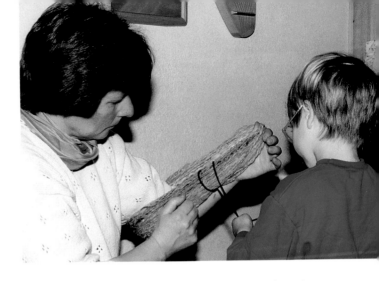

Before washing, bind the skein together loosely in four places

t-shirts of poor quality, where the left hand seam turns toward the front and the right one toward the back.

Threads can be twisted using a stone weight. Take some well-spun thread off a bobbin and divide it in half. Holding the ends of the thread in one hand, place a stone, scissors or other heavy object at the mid-point of the thread. When you release the heavy object, the two threads in your hand will turn very fast and twist themselves into a very strong two-ply string. Children often have a lot of ideas for things to make with this double thread.

Winding a skein

Winding a skein — a loosely-coiled bundle of yarn — is the simplest and best method to keep the twisted wool yarn ready for use.

Wind the yarn around your hand and elbow, and mark the end of the yarn with some thread of another colour so that the end can be found easily again later. Children who already under-stand something about numbers often enjoy counting the number of "elbows" it takes to wind the thread. Finally, bind the skein together loosely in four places.

Washing the yarn

When washing the yarn, handle it very carefully, as if you were handling a living creature. If children are told that it should be "bathed like a baby", they are normally especially careful. The yarn also doesn't like sudden changes in temperature, so ensure the water is just slightly warmer than lukewarm.

Place the yarn in water and gently move it back and forth, then hang it up to drip dry. Don't use any detergent because this reduces the natural oil content of the wool.

The drying process can be speeded up by rolling the yarn in towels, pressing it gently and then hanging the yarn to dry loosely in fresh air. It should never be dried in bright sunlight, when the temperature is below freezing, or in other extreme conditions. Turn it frequently so that moisture is able to escape from all over the skein.

Storage

After drying the wool, store it in an airy place, hanging it in skeins if possible. It should be well cared for, turned often, and kept with herb bags

If children wash the wool as gently as if they are bathing a baby, the wool will stay soft and loose

If the yarn is to be used soon, it can be rolled into a ball right away

to keep the moths away and to give the wool a nice fragrance. Lavender and cedar oil are good protection against moths. Remember that before the wool can be made into something, it must be wound into a ball.

Wool: from a Ball of Wool to a Toy Sheep

⁓ Finger crochet

For children, finger crochet is the simplest method of creating something from relatively rough and irregular hand-spun wool yarn. They can crochet for a long time and make extremely strong chains, using them as "horse reins", or bands to tie objects together, or to put a border around their play areas.

The following diagrams demonstrate the technique of finger crocheting:

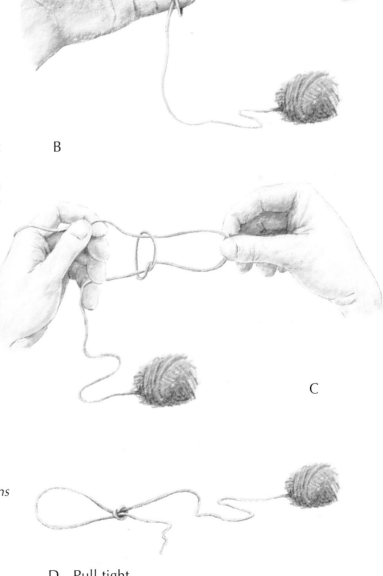

B

C

A, B, C, D = instructions for the basic loop

A

D   Pull tight

41

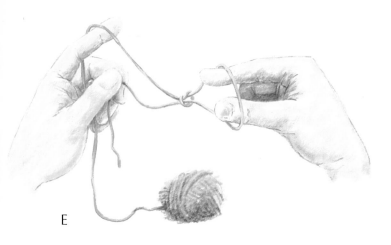

E

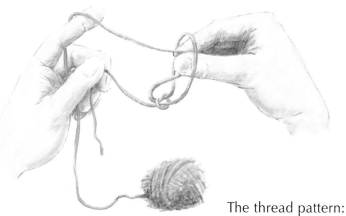

F

E and F can be repeated
as many times as you like

The thread pattern:

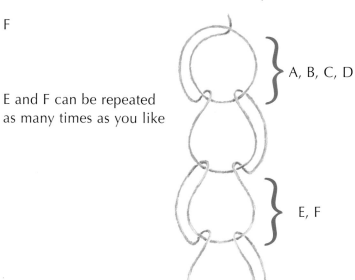

{ A, B, C, D

{ E, F

➤ *Weaving*

Weaving is a particularly good activity for children because there are so many options at different skill levels. Most children above the age of five enjoy weaving, if they're given looms and yarns which are appropriate for their level of motor development and powers of concentration. It can help to keep weaving activities of different skill levels in different physical spaces, to avoid confusion.

Looms made of cut and smoothly-sanded branches, nailed at the ends, and bound together with strong cord, strung with cotton warp yarn, and woven with plant-dyed sheep's wool

Stick table loom

The stick table loom, also known as the stick loom, consists of a 20 inch (50 cm) long base board, which is fastened to the table edge by two clamps. Wooden dowels are placed in 26 holes, each with a 3/8 inch (10.5 mm) diameter. Each dowel is 5 1/2 inches (135 mm) long and has a diameter of 3/8 inch (10 mm). The depth of the holes should be 5/8 inch (15 mm). Drill a 1/8 inch (3 mm) hole horizontally, about 6/8 inch (17 mm) from the end of the dowel for the warp thread, which is pulled through the holes.

Place the dowels into the holes of the base board and knot two warp thread pairs (four ends) together. At this point, the children can begin to weave: it is very easy for them to wind the yarn rhythmically back and forth.

When the full length of the dowels has been filled with weaving, remove the dowels from the base board and carefully press down on the woven rows; then replace the dowels onto the base board so that weaving can resume.

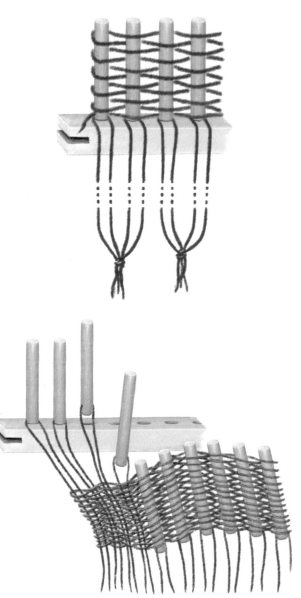

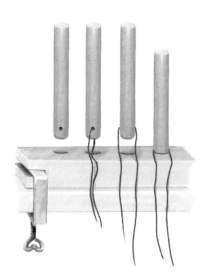

Thread spun on a stick spindle is ideal for weaving on a stick loom

Fast progress means the children stay interested for longer

Very long pieces of cloth can be made on stick looms: here the rug is 6 ft (2 m) long. Many hands push the finished strips toward the near end, doing so in pairs and at the same time from both sides. This way, the rug will be thick, strong and warm.

The advantage of this weaving method is that children can create any length of cloth from which rugs, cushion covers, etc. can be made.

Thick, hand-spun, twisted yarn is especially good for this kind of project. If the weaving yarn is too fine, the woven cloth may be too loose, and progress can be slow. It helps to work on the principle that the thicker the weaving yarn, the less impatient the child will become.

Stick looms can be made easily and cheaply. However, it is important to use a hardwood, such as beechwood: softer woods such as fir and pine split too easily, cannot be sanded as well, and are not solid enough.

CARDBOARD LOOM FRAME

Cardboard loom frames deserve a special mention because they can be individually made to match the skill of an individual child. Furthermore, the card used can be recycled from old calendars etc. — cheap, and environmentally friendly.

Make cuts in the ends of the cardboard about

Cardboard loom frames are easy to make and weaving progress is fast

3/4 inch (2 cm) long; you can vary the number of cuts and the space between between them. Pull the warp thread tight enough so that the cardboard is slightly curved, which gives the child a handy hollow space for weaving.

ROUNDED WOOD LOOM FRAME

Children often enjoy sawing, carving, sanding and then nailing together loom frames of notched wood.

Use rounded wood sticks, about 3/4 inch (2 cm) in diameter and any length. The wood should have been dried for a long time: with fresh, green wood, the corners of the loom can shrink, causing the frame to lose stability.

Cut two long and two short pieces. Carve notches into the ends, and sand all the pieces. Fit the indentations together and secure them with nails. Reinforce all four corners with very strong cord.

For the warp thread, either make small notches or drill fine holes in the two short pieces of the frame. The warp thread can then be pulled through the holes.

Notches like these produce very solid joints. Note that children will need help with this.

The corner joints are held together by nails and cord and warp thread is pulled through small drilled holes

CARD WEAVING

This technique can be used to weave belts, hair bands, key rings or bookmarks.

To make the weaving card, copy the pattern on page 47 onto strong cardboard and cut it out. Pull the warp thread through the card; the thread should be the right length for the piece of cloth you want to weave, plus 4–6 inches (10–15 cm) at each end.

Knot the ends of the warp threads together and attach one end to a hook, doorknob or similar object. Using string, attach the other end to the child's body.

Pull the moving set of warp threads to the top of the weaving card, and push the shuttle, also made of cardboard, through the space between the two sets of threads. Next, press the threads to the bottom of the card, and push the shuttle back through in the opposite direction. Repeat until your cloth is the desired length.

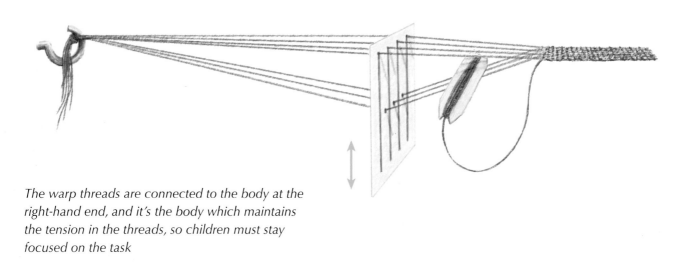

The warp threads are connected to the body at the right-hand end, and it's the body which maintains the tension in the threads, so children must stay focused on the task

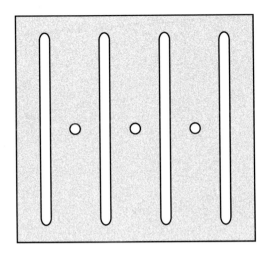

Copy the pattern onto strong cardboard and pull the warp threads through the three holes and four slits. Cut the shuttle out of cardboard as well, and wind the yarn around it.

Young weavers demonstrate their skills on a loom at a craft market

OTHER LOOMS AND WEAVING OPTIONS

There are endless options for weaving. The table-top loom (see picture on page 48), for example, is good for weaving fine, patterned cloth; this requires a higher level of skill, patience and dexterity. New ideas for weaving can often come from people with different cultural and ethnic backgrounds, or from museums.

◄ Weaving with the weaving card is good preparation for working with the floor loom

Weaving on a table-top loom. The girl is only seven years old, but she is already certain that she wants to become a weaver when she grows up.

— Knitting

From the age of about six, children enjoy learning to knit as long as they have the dexterity needed. In any case, thick needles, preferably made from sticks, are best, as well as strong yarn, hand-spun where possible.

To make knitting needles, take sticks that are about 1/4 inch (5–7 mm) thick and about 8 inches (20 cm) long. Twigs from hazel bushes work well. Sharpen them at one end with a pencil sharpener, then sand them until smooth. Glue a wooden bead or piece of cork to the other end to prevent the stitches from slipping off.

To make it easier to get started, and to make the knitting more stable, an adult should knit the first few rows.

Knitted cloth can be used to make many objects, including soft toys. See page 50 for a pattern for making a toy sheep. Experience shows that animals made with the children are especially well cared for.

A busy room: the motivation to weave is especially strong if the children have made their own looms

The finely sanded and sharpened knitting needle has a wooden bead on one end so that the stitches won't slip off

48

The farmer goes through

the gate,

pulls out a sheep

and closes the gate again

Every child should have a cuddly sheep! It can be knitted using the pattern on page 50, and stuffed with carded sheep's wool.

Even the oldest kindergarten children love playing with home-made soft farm animals

Toy sheep pattern

Using the pattern below as a guide, make the individual sections from knitted or crocheted fabric, or simply cut them out from existing cloth which is not too soft. You'll need two of the 'side of the head' pieces, four ear sections and one 'top of the head' piece. (The muzzle is not really necessary; you can decide to use it or not when you're sewing the pieces together and stuffing the head.) The ear pieces can be lined with silk. The tail can be made from a piece of twisted wool cord that is 2½–3 inches (6–8 cm) long. Wooden buttons make good eyes.

Sew the stomach section and the back section together at the feet and legs, and along each side of the belly (photograph 1 on page 51 clearly shows the feet and belly seams). Cut open a slit in the sheep's back to allow for stuffing the main body and legs, then sew up afterwards (photograph 2 on page 51 shows the seam running down the back of the sheep).

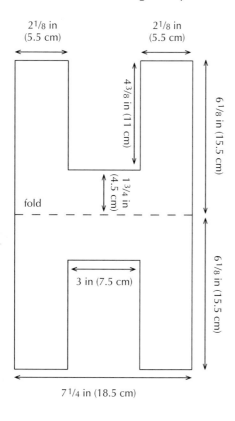

Stomach section

The marked fold runs down the centre of the stomach, on the underside of the sheep

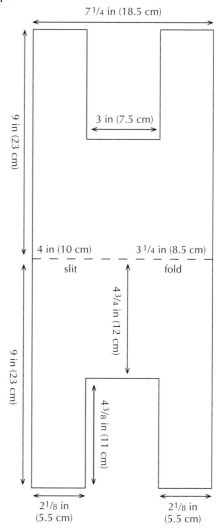

Back section

The marked fold runs down the back of the sheep

50

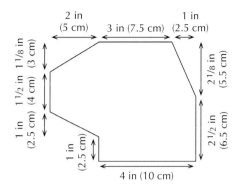

Side of the head (two pieces required)

When stuffing the legs, be careful to stuff further than the stomach line, or the legs will bend too easily. A few stitches with a long needle back and forth through the stomach, and from the head to the tail, can help the sheep keep its shape.

For the head, sew the two 'side of the head' sections together along the top and bottom seams, and sew in the 'top of the head' section between them so that the head comes to a triangular point at the nose (photograph 1 below shows the front of the head). Stuff the head and attach it to the body; note that head naturally sits slightly sideways, with one of the ears higher than the other.

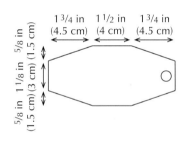

Top of the head

Muzzle (optional)

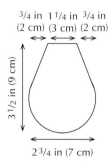

Ear (four pieces required)

1. Underside of sheep

2. Side of sheep

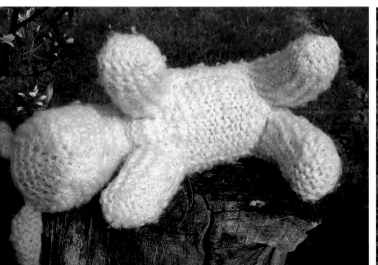

— Felt

Making felt from wool is one of the oldest known textile techniques, familiar in many countries around the world. Fabric can be produced faster this way than by spinning, weaving, crocheting or knitting.

Anyone can make felt, but patience is needed to succeed. It is a process that trains perseverance! Children around the ages of four and five particularly enjoy splashing around with soapsuds and wool.

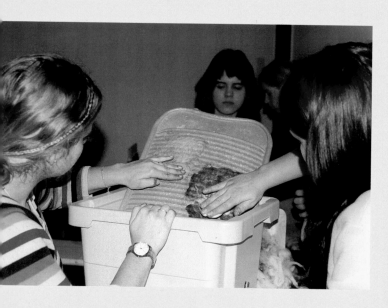

First attempts at making felt from raw wool in hot soapsuds

Making dry felt from sheep's wool is fun for even the youngest children. Wool picked off fences during a country walk and played with soon becomes a very small, dense lump of wool in a child's damp, sweaty hands (remember to wash hands before eating your sandwiches). They soon realize that much nicer things can be made from wool if soapsuds are used, and colour is added.

Only small objects should be made with children — balls, beads and friendship bracelets — because these things can be finished fairly quickly. Larger pieces require more patience and are better for adults.

MAKING FELT BALLS

Make a small, tight core out of raw wool, and then wrap a layer of plain carded wool around the core. The carded layer must be carefully pulled apart, and should not be twisted. Add a final thin layer of coloured wool. Here too the fibres should be smooth and loose, otherwise the wool will not stick together. The wool ball should be the right size to fit in a child's hand.

Roll the dry ball until the hair ends begin to hook into each other. Then wet the child's hands with soapsuds (1 tablespoon of soap to 1 litre or quart of water), so the ball can be turned between the palms of the hands.

The child then wets and turns the ball alternately. The wool should not stick to the child's hands; if this happens, not enough soapsuds are being used.

To begin with, the ball should only be turned, not squeezed. After a while the soapsuds soak the entire ball, and when the outer layer has become more stable, more pressure can be applied. The soapsuds should be around 104–122°F (40–50°C), and the ball can start to be dipped into them occasionally. Keep working and don't become impatient. Making felt requires perseverance.

Place the wool balls onto a towel on a table and roll them until they are solid. This will produce a tight ball which should then be washed in clear, cold water.

Felt balls have many uses. A walnut shell containing a few grains or small pebbles can be worked into the middle of a felt ball, to make a pleasing sound when shaken.

To make a felt apple, use apple-coloured wool for the outer layer. Pull the ball into an apple shape by sewing a strong thread through the middle to compress it slightly. To finish, sew on a small stem and leaf.

Small felt balls attached to tight threads make wonderful necklaces and they go well with friendship bracelets in matching colours.

FRIENDSHIP BRACELETS

To make a friendship bracelet, take a ribbon of carded wool about 12 inches (30 cm) long and about 3/8 inch (1 cm) thick when pressed, and roll it back and forth with wet hands in soapsuds. Form the wool into a tight sausage until no fibres can be pulled out, then knot the ends together to form a bracelet of the right size.

Multi-coloured bracelets can be made this way as well: the only limit is your imagination! Unique pieces of jewelry can be created using two or three colours; the initial wool ribbons can also be knotted or braided together before they are felted for different effects.

Marianne Frielingsdorf, nature teacher

⌐ *Magic Wool*

Wool that has been cleaned, finely carded and dyed is often called "magic wool" or "fairy wool" and can be bought from specialists shops (see Craft suppliers at the end of the book). If possible, of course, it's better for children to see the whole process of producing such wool, right from the sheep.

Before dyeing wool, make sure it's completely clean. Ideally, the process of soaking the wool in rainwater or well-water, beating it, drying it and pulling it apart should be repeated five to ten times, and can take from one to three weeks.

The procedure for dyeing wool is the same as for dyeing silk or cotton. (A basic description of dyeing cloth can be found in the *Spring* book in this series, along with a table of plant dye colours.) With wool, however, you need to work at higher temperatures, and allow a longer time for steeping and dyeing. Wool that has not yet been carded can also be dyed, and it can be fun to let the children experiment.

Carded wool fleece that has been dyed with plant colours

Plant dyes are harder to come by in winter because we're not able to harvest plants there and then, and must rely on those collected during the previous summer. In an emergency, plant dyes can be purchased from craft supply shops; alternatively, in winter try a dye bath made from onion skins.

After steeping, rinsing, dyeing and drying the wool, card it enough that it becomes soft and fluffy, earning it the name "fairy wool". It now has many uses:

- ❀ Young children like to just look at it and feel it
- ❀ It can be used to create colourful wool pictures or wall hangings, on a background of felt or burlap. This kind of activity is an ideal cross-generational project, suitable for every-

These figures made from unspun dyed sheep's wool are for a puppet play

Environmentally-sound houses filled with fairy-tale dolls

Simple, wound wool dolls made from fairy wool

one from four years old to one hundred and four.

* It can be used to make felt, as described above
* Various human and animal shapes can be made from it, with or without a "skeleton", to cuddle and play with in a doll's house or farm, or to form puppets for fairy-tale plays.

There are lots of things to make with magic wool, and there are some excellent books on the subject (see Resources at the end of the book).

Free Play with Wool

There are many opportunities for free play in a wool workshop. Children often associate wool with snowflakes, and white wool can start to float through the air. Sometimes, children cover themselves from head to toe with wool fleece and pretend to hibernate, like plants under the snow. This way they experience the special warmth and quality of the wool.

Some children like to fall into the wool basket or a pile of wool fleece. They feel comfortable, safe and warm there. A six-year-old girl who, in freezing outdoor temperatures, was dressed in synthetic leggings, a cotton sweatshirt, and thin socks told us after the first hour of work in the wool workshop that, for the first time in her life, she had warm hands.

Stories

Telling children fairy tales and stories which fit in with the projects they're doing can add a new dimension to their experience, by communicating

After working, children like to lie down and rest

on an emotional level. There are several Grimm's fairy tales suitable for use in a wool workshop (see Further Reading at the end of the book for sources of these stories):

* A Pack of Ragamuffins
* Rumpelstiltskin
* Mother Holle
* The Spindle, the Shuttle and the Needle
* The Three Spinners

Experience has shown that the children want to hear the fairy tales at least three times, and preferably more; it helps them to connect with the mood of the story, and relate to it better.

February

Working with Willow

Woodworking

It is during February that the first signs of spring appear. Life-giving water soaks plant seeds and roots as the snow melts and heavy rains come. Our ancestors represented this in the zodiac with Aquarius, the Water Bearer (♒): Aquarius pours his vessels, filled with the water of life, over the earth.

Towards the end of February, under the zodiac sign of Pisces, the Fish (♓), buds begin to appear on perennials, trees and bushes as water rises in the plants, and the sun's power increases. The fish is a perfect symbol for the strong impulse in nature to multiply and spread: under the right conditions, fish breed in huge numbers. Thousands of fish eggs are fertilised and serve as valuable nourishment to other creatures.

In the plant world, tiny delicate root ends break through seed shells and find support, strength and security in the earth. The days start to become longer and birds begin to sing in the morning and evening, reminding us to think about building nesting boxes for them (see the *Spring* book in this series).

The increasing warmth of the sun also tempts bees out from their winter rest. Up until now, they have hung, in a bunch, near their queen, close to the winter honey store which sustains them

A nesting aid for bumblebees. The fragrance of the honey water in the Lego blocks make the site especially attractive, and is a welcome source of nourishment for the queen.

A nesting aid for bumblebees

through the cold months. The first flight out is their chance to get rid of the waste products that have built up: it is known as the cleansing flight.

Snowdrops, crocuses, crowfoot and other early blooming flowers act as a visual invitation for the bees. As soon as the last snow has melted, the bumblebee queen will start the search for a nesting place.

Working with Willow

Building Houses from Hedges

February: the Last Chance to Cut Willow

February is the best time for working with willows. This can only be done, however, if the ground is no longer frozen and is not too wet. In some places, such as Germany, this is the last chance to cut willows because after March 1

they are officially protected, so that their catkins can provide nourishment for bees. Even if it's not restricted in your country, it's still good practice to cut willow earlier in the season. Pollarded willows will attract birds looking for a good location to build their nest.

Willow: a Good Plant for Children

The willow is a good plant for children to work with. It grows so fast that you can almost see it

Old, well cared-for pollarded willows in swampy areas not only have a fantastic, expressive shape, but also supply huge amounts of willow branches

Although only a few bare willow branches have been put together vertically and horizontally, the children immediately have a sense of space and furnish the new "house"

Sleep, Thou Little Willow Tree

1 Sleep, thou lit - tle wil - low tree, through the win - ter weath - er
2 Gen - tle winds shall cra - dle thee, and the sun watch o'er thee,

with the blue - bell and the rose, with the birch and heath - er.
till the spring shall make the flow'rs bow their heads be - fore thee.

Wait un - til the sun is bright, and the row - an blos - soms white.
Then put off your sil - ver down, don your shin - ing gold - en gown.

Sleep, thou lit - tle wil - low tree, through the win - ter weath - er.
Gen - tle winds shall cra - dle thee, and the sun watch o'er thee.

grow. Its shoots are soft and flexible and its velvety catkins are soft, just asking to be touched.

Willows take root in the ground almost visibly. Children can watch this happen: fill a large jar with sand, pebbles and water, stick a willow branch in the jar, and watch the roots grow.

If the area is not too dry, plant willows in every garden where there are children. In February, the willows will blossom.

Willow: Creative Possibilities

February is often the time when hedges are trimmed along roads or streams. Don't be afraid to ask whoever is locally responsible for this work if you can have some of the willow branches they cut. These branches are valuable in making everything from huts to fences.

Willow projects are good opportunities for people of different ages to work together. Children as

From the simple little fence made of curved branches ...

... to a loosely woven high fence ...

... through tightly woven branches to secure a slope ...

... to a woven dome above a seat in a willow hut.
Willow offers so many different creative possibilities.

young as three and four can participate: from experience, they especially like carrying the cuttings to the planting holes, or using their little wheelbarrows, toy trucks and buckets to move sand around. They also enjoy watering the plants to make them grow big and strong.

Care must be taken when willow branches are being woven because it's easy for them to spring

A domed gate made of willow. As soon as the snow has melted, branches can be bound or woven. ➤

back and hit someone in the face. Ensure that there is always sufficient space between everyone working on the project, and protect the eyes with goggles.

The *Spring* and *Autumn* books in this series contain more activities which use willow. The following pictures show a few examples of what can be achieved.

If, during the winter, a ring of willow branches is added to a dome of willows, in the spring the newly growing shoots can be braided into the dome. In the summer there will then be a lovely "sky window" in the roof of the dome.

Making a Latticework Willow Hedge

Willow hedges used as living fences are a good way to divide outdoor areas into playing spaces and rest spaces for children. At the Children's Nature and Garden Centre we built this kind of fence near the beehive next to the road. We

2. Trim the small twigs off the selected willow branches, which should be 6.5 ft (2 m) long and 2 inches (5 cm) in diameter, and as straight as possible

3. Lay the willow branches in a diagonal grid at the desired intervals. Strip the bark from the branches where they cross each other.

4. Secure these crossing points with screws

1. To begin constructing a latticework willow hedge, dig a ditch as deep as possible

wanted to encourage the bees to fly off at a certain height in order to protect them from the dangers of passing vehicles. In addition, the hedge protects them with its leaves during the summer. In the spring, the catkins offer the bees an early source of nourishment.

5. Carefully cut a long strip of bark from the ends of the branches that will be put into the ditch. This will enable the branches to absorb water better.

6. Put the bound branch structure into the ditch and water well before the ditch has been filled with earth, so that the cuttings will get a good start in developing their roots

Woodworking

Wood: a Valuable Material

As the days grow longer in February, the sap begins to rise in the trees and bushes. In our part of the world it has been the custom for thousands of years to cut the wood we need in the days before spring arrives. Trees and bushes are as if they have been "freeze-dried" by the winter frost. This means that the wood can be relatively easily processed and moved, and is also much lighter than when it is filled with sap. Wood cut in February also burns well.

In addition, we do most woodcutting before the end of February because later on the woods and hedges are nurseries for the animal and plant worlds and we don't want to disturb the life developing there.

Piles of firewood are rare these days. Activities are even more fun if different generations work together.

Works of art found in nature

houses, fences and vehicles were built of wood. Most heat came from burning wood. Wood was used for musical instruments, bark for tanning and branches for basket-weaving; nothing was thrown away, not even the smallest twigs which kept the fire going in the baking oven.

For generations, people wisely planted forests for their grandchildren but in our present hi-tech age, we feel that we cannot manage without many synthetically-produced materials. In some areas of our lives, however, wood — a renewable resource that presents no recycling problems — could very well be used again. Fortunately, more people are starting to think like this.

Our consumer rubbish or garbage is easy to get rid of, even if we have to first sort it into recycling bags. We have a tendency to throw out our conscience at the same time as throwing out the rubbish, whereas in reality, that's where a lot of our ecological problems start. For the sake of our planet and future generations, we must reduce the amount of rubbish we produce; and for that, we must all take personal responsibility for our lifestyles.

When working with children, we can go a long way towards instilling these kinds of values. If they learn to work with natural materials now, they're more likely to look for natural alternatives later in life.

Forests are often viewed these days as simply economic commodities, rather than as life-giving ecosystems. Our mass-production of wood means that many forests are in a bad state, plagued by bark beetles and other pests which must be combatted with toxic chemicals. We've lost sight of forests as a key link in the chain of earth, water, light and air.

Years ago, all the wood that was cut found a good use. It supported many aspects of human life: furniture, tools, kitchen equipment, wooden shoes and many other useful objects. Entire

66

One of the things we've forgotten is that a healthy forest stores a huge amount of water. Diseased trees mean diseased roots, which can have a serious effect on local water and, in turn, on global water supplies. Our climates seem increasingly to suffer from the extremes of flooding and drought; if we're to reverse these kind of changes, trees will be an important part of the process.

The Beech Tree's Guests

Four fine tenants in its house
Has the ancient beech tree.
In the cellar lives the mouse;
Who else can we see?

Proudly with his shining coat
And store of nuts and seeds,
Here, the first-floor gentleman,
Mr Squirrel, feeds.

Further up the woodpecker
Has his place for working.
He chops and pounds precisely,
Wood chips flying nicely.

In the branches at the top
Pipes a songbird sweetly.
The beech tree is a perfect home
And all the guests live cheaply.

Rudolf Baumbach

Forests

Wood is a sustainable, living material which in early times filled our living spaces. Today, we can still find many varieties of wood in old buildings such as farmhouses:

- floors and rafters of fir, which can survive for three hundred years
- beams from nine hundred-year-old oaks, which can be reused even after a fire
- roof tiles from larches, which can resist the weather for centuries
- a variety of furniture, for example, from pine and cherry wood
- craftsmen's posts and ships' masts from elastic ash wood
- firewood from the beech tree that stores warmth and gives off heat
- many other objects such as musical instruments and children's toys from specially selected types of wood

In a healthy forest, 4–13 cubic yards (3–10 cubic metres) of wood can grow per hectare (10 000 square metres or 2.5 acres) in the course of a year, depending on the quality of the earth. In managed forests, only the amount of wood that is able to grow back, is cut down. It is important to manage our forests well, because of their huge influence on our environment. For example, forests store large amounts of water in moderate and tropical climates, so that during droughts there are reserves for farming and energy needs. Forests also support permanently fertile areas for farming and gardening, contribute to the cleansing of the air, and give off large amounts of oxygen. If we look after them, they'll look after us!

A wooden animal toy — as if it grew by itself ...

In many areas, forests shelter a wide range of rare plants and animal species, and biodiversity is to be encouraged as much as possible. Forests also serve as recreation and relaxation spaces for people who live in cities and urban areas.

The history of forests on our planet shows that our mismanagement of them has led not only to infertile soil but to some areas becoming permanent deserts. We should have learned that forests with a single species such as fir or pine forests are significantly less healthy than mixed forests of many species, which are much better at cleansing their environment and resisting infection.

- mixed forests are better at filtering harmful substances from the air
- mixed forests more effectively protect groundwater from becoming acidic, and from other pollution
- mixed forests show a remarkable resistance to bark beetles and damage from ice and storms

Planting of biologically-diverse permanent forests is therefore a key aspect of future forestry.

Great changes in our weather and environment are currently threatening our forests. A recent environmental conference in Nairobi, Kenya, reported that 55 000 hectares (222 acres) of virgin forest are being destroyed every day around the world. Dying forest areas have expanded into virgin forests and national parks, and every year large areas of forests fall victim to bark beetles, ice and storms. Many species of trees are threatened by extreme weather conditions and climate change.

We need to develop new, forward-looking forestry methods in order to restore our forests for the twenty-first century:

- "Natural forestry," that is, forestry which is economically, socially and environmentally sustainable, has been carried out in both private and state initiatives for the last twenty years. Every year, more and more monoforests of fir and pine are being changed into mixed forest.
- Since 1969, new methods of tree regeneration have been researched using biodynamic methods of forestry. This means that the cosmic relationships between different species are taken into consideration in planting.
- An increasing number of breeding gardens and model forests are appearing in moderate, tropical and subtropical regions.

Older children can learn about reforestation methods through placements and courses with forestry organisations such the Forestry Commission (UK), Irish Natural Forestry Foundation or the American Forest Foundation.

Georg W. Schmidt, ecologist

Children especially treasure toys they've seen being made

Wooden Toys

Children's rooms today are often filled with objects with which the children have no real relationship. Modern mass-produced toys can stifle children's imagination, do nothing to satisfy a child's desire for real-life experiences, and present a distorted image of the world and human beings. These factors can result in disorientation for the child, and a startling loss of core values. How can we even start to tackle these problems?

The important thing is to start. We need to pass on a love of wood and natural materials to our children, and this shouldn't be hard: the relationship between people and nature is already strong. Collect a small supply of wood when you're out and about, and inspire children with what they can learn, and what can be made, from wood.

Children feel a deep relationship with toys that have been made in their presence and with their help. The toys will be handled carefully and treasured much more than anonymous mass-produced toys. In addition, working with wood stimulates

Listening to Wood

Practical activity has always been, and will continue to be, a basic human need. This is especially true for children: practical activity is how they develop imagination, observation skills, perseverance, care and ideas, which will benefit them throughout their lives.

Working with wood is like having a conversation with a growing work of art. Wood is very special among natural materials: as a growing thing, even after being shaped it still has life. Recognising this is an important first step. If we talk to the wood, and listen carefully with all our senses, it will tell us about its hardness, weight and flexibility. It invites us to follow the direction of its growth, its grain and branches, first with our eyes, then with our hands, and finally with our tools. Then we'll see if we've understood the wood correctly. With every stroke of our hands, our developing piece of wood should remain what it was originally: a growing work of art.

Our questions to the wood should be: what are you like? How should I handle you? Tell me about your specific personality. These questions can apply equally when dealing with plants, animals or indeed other people.

If we treat wood with love, it will love us back.

Christian Tangemann, social worker

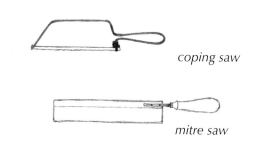
coping saw

mitre saw

foxtail saw

At the beginning of each workshop, place the tools into a neat circle, name them while placing them, and then play a game. One child leaves the room; a tool is removed or placed in another spot and the child must then try to guess what has changed.

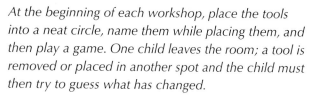
bow saw

children's imagination and helps them to gain fine motor skills.

⌐ Tools

Kindergarten children should experience the physical qualities of wood directly, with their own hands and bodies. Once they're older, they will be able to handle sharp and electrical tools safely, understand their principles and feel the connection between their energy and the tool's function.

Tools suitable for slightly older kindergarten children (age six or seven) include rough and fine saws, hand drills, hammers, pliers, screwdrivers, files and mitre boxes. A variety of clamps can be useful as well. For adults or school-age children (seven and older), other tools can be available, such as awls for making holes, chisels, carving knives, mallets and garden shears. A tool such as a wooden mallet can itself be made in a wood workshop, before being used there.

carving knife

wood or leather mallet

rasp or file

stick chisel

hollow chisel

angular hollow chisel

A mix of purchased and hand-made tools: mallets, awls, chisels and files

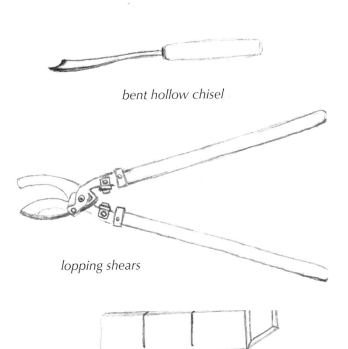

bent hollow chisel

lopping shears

mitre box

brace and bit

screw awl

hand drill

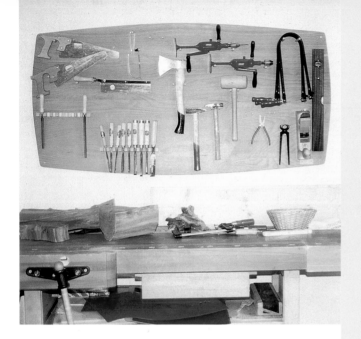

Tool wall in a Waldorf kindergarten

Tools, either purchased or hand-made, have their own value and should be treated with care. Drawing an outline of each tool on the wall where it hangs will help keep things in their rightful places.

Little birds and other toys made from twigs

⌐ Carving twigs in kindergarten

This is an account of a twig-carving workshop in a local kindergarten.

The children gathered in the kindergarten playground, and the kindergarten teacher said: "All children who will be starting school next year, get a chair. Today, we're going to carve something together."

A circle of chairs quickly formed. In the middle, the teacher spread out a colourful cloth and placed various tools on it: simple knives and kitchen knives with wooden handles in a box, garden shears, small hand drills, sandpaper, and a box on which a red cross was painted.

"Now children," said the teacher, "place your hands on your hips and sit far enough apart so that you don't touch your neighbour, because for carving you need a lot of room. Now hold your hands in front of you and move your fingers. Who can wiggle them really fast? What do you see here? The best tools of all are your hands. With them you can do almost everything, they are always with you, and you can't lose them.

"For some jobs, however, we need simple tools such as a knife for carving, a drill for drilling, or saws for sawing. We can't perform these jobs with our own fingers, but tools will help us. They are here on the cloth, sorted into groups. Look at them carefully. Now close your eyes. Now open your eyes. What has changed? That's right, one of the saws is now between the drills. Well done!

"Each of you take a knife out of the box when I come around. Remember that they are sharp so be careful. Let's look at the knives. They have a wooden handle, like the knives in your kitchen, and a blade. The blade has two edges. One edge

72

is wider and you can run your finger carefully over that edge; that is the back of the knife. The other edge is the cutting edge; never run your fingers over that edge, because it is very sharp. When working, always hold only the handle and always carve toward the middle of the circle of chairs, never towards your neighbour.

"If you are not carving and want to stand up, lay the knife on your chair. Never walk around with the knife in your hand! If you remember all of these important rules, we might not need the sticking plasters from the box with the red cross.

"I've collected some branches and twigs in the garden and woods. Tomorrow we'll do this together, but we must never break off fresh branches, because then the trees and bushes will cry.

"In this branch here, with a lot of knots, little birds are hiding, with a tiny head, a tail, and tiny legs. We want to look for them. Who has discovered one?"

The teacher points to a little girl.

"This is the tail, that's the head with the beak, and here are the legs. This bird is singing and chirping," says the little girl.

"Very good," says the teacher. "Now you." She points to a little boy.

"There's the head with the beak; here is the tail, and those are the legs. It has just discovered a seed on the ground and is picking it up," says the little boy.

"Excellent," says the teacher. "Now we'll take the garden shears and cut off all the wood that doesn't fit the little birds we've found. I'll help you if it's hard. For now, we'll leave the legs as they are. On the head we'll carve a sharp beak and make the tail thinner above and below, so that the bird is lighter and can fly better.

"At the moment, we can only hold the bird in our hands or lay it down, but birds need to be able to stand on their legs when they sing and pick up seeds. We'll saw a round disc from an elderberry branch, because this piece of wood already has a hole in it. Can you see the hole? Smooth the disc well with sandpaper. Now, hold the bird by its legs, think up a magic saying, and stick the legs into the natural hole in the wooden disc. If soft pith shows at the bottom, you can take that out. Now we know how big the legs have to be. If the legs are too thick, carve them to be thinner; if they are too thin, we can use a piece of wood as a wedge. Later on you can use chestnuts, beeswax, or clay as a stand. Now, go to work!"

Christian Tangemann, social worker

The wooden horse and its rider are a firm favourite if they've been made by hand

Building blocks like these can be made by the oldest kindergarten children: they can saw them and sand them themselves. The depth of the wood grain can be enhanced with a natural stain or sealant.

⌐ Fences and railings

Once children have mastered some basic tools, they can move on to creating all kinds of fences and railings for a toy farm or zoo.

Children love to join in when they see stick dolls emerging from round pieces of wood, chicks from twigs, boats from bark or a crane from a branch

Fences that aren't glued can be changed again and again, challenging a child's dexterity and imagination

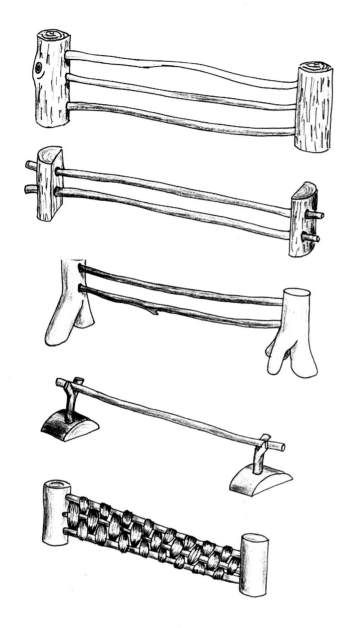

- Sand all the individual pieces until they're beautifully smooth
- Treat all the finished pieces with a natural oil: linseed oil or beeswax work well
- The fences and railings can be glued for extra strength; alternatively, leaving them unglued gives children greater flexibility to make changes to the scene later on (in this case, make the drilled holes a bit larger)

⌐ Doll's houses and furniture

Children often enjoy making miniature furniture for a hand-made doll's house from knotted branches.

- To make a chair, saw a branch on a diagonal (a small saw is best for this) then carve out a hollow for sitting and sand it well

The walls of these doll's houses (see also next page) are made of plywood. They can be adjusted into different arrangements of rooms and easily folded together after playing. The furniture is carved from knotted branches; it can be made by older children who have some experience in working with wood, but this activity is best done with an adult helping.

- Use round pieces of wood, forked branches, or pieces of dowling, and saw them to size
- If necessary, split the round pieces of wood length-ways with a kitchen knife and a small hammer
- Drill holes for the joints using a hand drill or a spiral drill

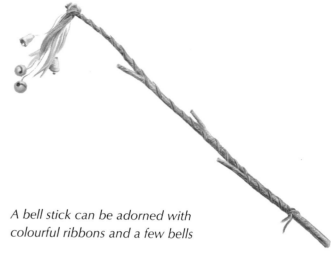

- ❀ A table or stool can be made from a section of a branch that has been finely sanded and sealed or waxed
- ❀ When making a bench, carve the base flat so that the bench will sit straight. Then saw the seat and arms at the correct angle, along the length of the grain.
- ❀ Each piece should be finely sanded, so that it feels good in the child's hand

A bell stick can be adorned with colourful ribbons and a few bells

Rattles and Stick Instruments to Scare away Winter

In days gone by, people celebrated Candlemas on February 2 to mark the lengthening of the days. If you had neither electricity, heat nor lamps, the desire to get rid of dark winter, and to welcome the increasing light, was very strong. Driving out winter (and evil spirits, witches and demons) with bells, rattles, flutes and other loud instruments was common, helped along by colourful masks and costumes.

Children love carnivals, and a "driving out winter" ceremony is a great excuse to introduce

A bell ring can be made of thin willow or hazelnut branches, wound with crepe paper, and decorated with silk ribbons. The little bells are attached with strong yarn or silver wire.

The stick rattle is carved out of hazelnut wood. Carve or saw notches into a straight, thin branch, about 1 foot (30 cm) long and 1 in (2.5 cm) thick. Rub a thinner stick back and forth along the grooves to make noise.

"Fools" in action during the carnival season

This rattle consists of two discs made of soft wood with holes into which thin dowels have been glued. Put a round bell inside before gluing the rods.

some colour and noise to the end of the season. Children can be involved in making instruments such as sticks that can be rapped together, rings, rattles and bells, all adorned with colourful flying ribbons.

This graceful water castle, created from hard root wood, was made by craft teachers for a seminar project. It is a natural work of art with great play value in the sandbox.

"It almost sounds right," said this girl, as she played an imaginary violin made of roots with a wire brush

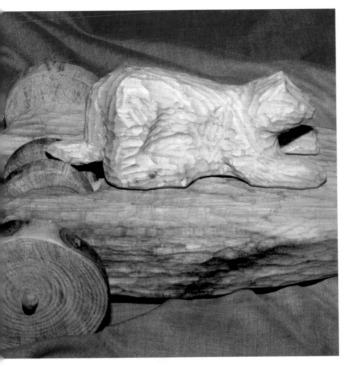 

Unique pieces of wood can help individual children to realize their talents. This is a movable cat and mouse toy, carved by a ten-year-old girl for younger children

Children have worked very hard on this piece of fir with a rotten core, to keep the natural beauty of the branches inside intact

More woodworking projects

All kinds of wood material can be used for woodworking: trunk or branch sections in various sizes, forked branches, pieces of bark, parts of hollow trees, roots and Christmas tree tops, to name but a few. Unique special pieces that appeal to us are worth caring for and keeping. In today's throwaway society, we should make an effort to treasure naturally-grown material and the work involved. The following pictures offer examples of things that can be made from wood — but of course the possibilities are endless. Use your imagination!

With an adult's help, children can build a home for small animals (see the Spring book for details)

▲ Making owl houses out of tree trunks with rotten cores ▼

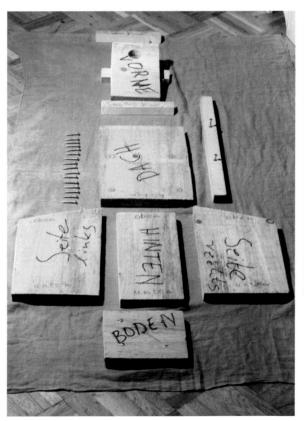

◄ An important aspect of the wood workshop in February is the creation of houses for various kinds of birds. The best method is to have the children take apart a carefully-made nesting box in order to gain a good sense of the individual parts. The parts can then be used as a pattern to copy (see the Spring book for details).

This boy is sharpening supports with an axe; the wood will be used to build a play ditch

▲ Older children with lots of energy can be put to work on a sawhorse

If you want to become an expert, you must start practising early ... ➤

... and it takes a lot of practice to hit a nail on the head

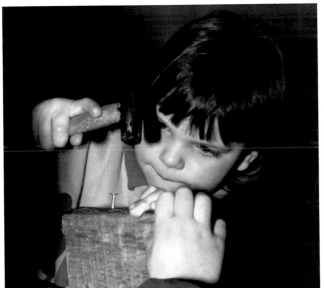

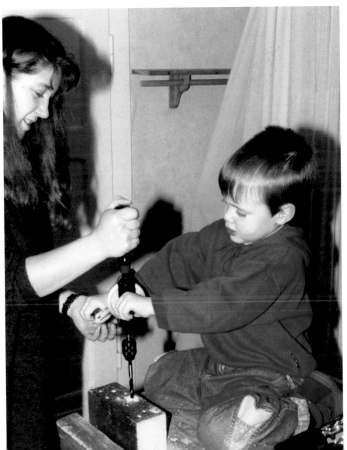

This is Johannes Brenner, who has a medieval portable lathe. He demonstrates how to equip simply-furnished weatherproof, rustic woodworking areas for children with sawhorses, clamp benches and portable lathes. This is a clamp bench with an attached sawhorse; the wood is prepared here then turned on a lathe.

A roof tile is prepared with a draw knife on the clamp bench

These nutcrackers come from his workshop, but children can make simpler shapes

These horses were created during a project week at a Steiner-Waldorf school, where children of different ages worked together. Branches of different thicknesses were joined together to make simple forms — and the children couldn't be happier playing on the backs of them.

Scrap lumber can also be used for building

83

February

Working with Clay

Clay

Pottery: a Valuable Activity

Creating things with clay is a basic craft activity which is good for all children to do, especially those with behavioural or psychological difficulties who need particular attention.

Making pottery has been part of human history for almost as long as we know. Archaeologists have discovered clay objects all over the world, many made using the same techniques as we use today: that is, by hand.

Our hands are incredibly important, and serve many purposes from gesturing and expressing our innermost feelings, to being excellent tools. Using hands to work with clay, then, should be included in the curriculum of every kindergarten and school as a basic experience of childhood. Through touching and moulding clay with their hands, children learn about key concepts such as smooth and rough, damp and dry, inside and outside. Having hands-on experience with opposites such as these can help children centre and orient themselves. Clay has a good mix of characteristics which can lead to focused, contented activity, even in normally restless children.

Clays are a mixture of minerals such as kaolin, montmorillonite, betonite and quartz. They are formed when stone containing feldspar or other silicates decomposes, and the residue becomes a sediment in calm water. Mixed with other mineral substances, they are usually gray, black or reddish brown.

In February, outdoor play can still be limited by bad weather and darkness, so working with clay gives children an activity involving a natural, outdoor material that can be carried out indoors: the perfect combination for this time of year.

Basic Rules for Doing Pottery with Children

❀ Creating objects from clay is relatively time-consuming due to the necessary drying and firing time. For this reason, begin the work early.

❀ For every clay object, cut a round disc from cardboard and place under the clay; this prevents the clay from sticking to the table while it is being shaped or dried

❀ Make clay available as often as possible and in large quantities in tubs or, better yet, as a pile. Children should not work too long with clay in cooler weather, because it extracts too much warmth from their hands.

❀ Small amounts of clay can be formed into balls, packed in wet cloths or foil, and placed on the radiator for several hours before beginning work; the clay will then not be so cold

❀ Fire simple clay objects as follows:
  • Place the objects into the kiln
  • Slowly heat the kiln to 1740°F (950°C)
  • Continue the firing
  • Slowly heat the kiln to 2190°F (1200°C)

Clay Bowls for Easter Grass

Spring is coming, and clay bowls and pots are needed to plant flowers and Easter grass in March (see the *Spring* book for more information).

Use a lump of clay about the size of a large apple (keeping in mind the size of the child's hands) for an Easter grass bowl. Make a nice smooth ball, and it place it on a cardboard disc. It's good to start by teaching a pinch pot tech-

▲ When dividing the clay into portions, keep in mind the size of the children's hands. They should be able to surround the portion with both hands.

Sowing wheat seeds in earth-filled Easter grass bowls

nique: the right thumb presses a hollow into the ball, while the left hand presses against the ball. This way the child can feel, and alter, the thickness of the bowl. In fact, pressure from the inside and outside along with rhythmical turning is the secret to making all round vessels. If the outer surface splits, it can be smoothed over with wet fingers or a knife or spatula.

When the bowls have dried a bit, tap the bottoms carefully upwards to make them flat, so that the finished bowl won't wobble. Place them onto newspaper or cardboard in a space protected from drafts and extreme temperature changes, and leave to dry for seven to fourteen days, depending on the thickness of the bowls. In this raw state, the bowls are very fragile and can break easily, so they need to be handled as carefully as raw eggs.

Finally, fire the Easter bowls as described on page 86. The high temperatures make the bowls so hard that they let almost no moisture through, so it's not necessary to glaze them. This is known as sintering.

Making a bird bath can be communal activity

Clay Insect Nests and Bird Baths

As a natural material, clay is very well suited to making nesting boxes for solitary insects such as hermit bees, bumblebees and wasps who naturally live in old wood. Drill holes between $1/8$ and $3/8$ inches wide (3 and 10 mm) into clay nests, drilling as deeply as possible. The insects will use them during the warm season.

Bird baths can also be made from clay. It is important to keep the edges low, and to build up a small mound in the middle so the birds can use it for both bathing and drinking. Use a firing temperature of 1200°C (2190°F) to make the bird bath partially frost-resistant. Children will enjoy filling the bird bath with fresh water, and this is a good opportunity to teach small children that our protection of nature depends on reliable, continuous care. It's never too early for children to learn this.

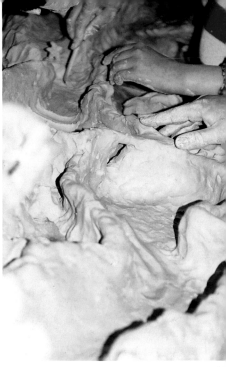

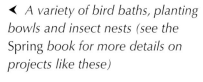

▲ Nests for solitary insects such as hermit bees, bumblebees and wasps

▲ Many hands are involved in building a table-top landscape from clay

◄ A variety of bird baths, planting bowls and insect nests (see the Spring book for more details on projects like these)

◄ Clay activities are suitable and popular all year round

Resources

Further reading

— General

Freya Jaffke, *Celebrating Festivals with Children*, Floris Books, Edinburgh

Freya Jaffke, *Work and Play in Early Childhood*, Floris Books, Edinburgh

Sally Jenkinson, *The Genius of Play*, Hawthorn Press, Stroud

Martin Large, *Set Free Childhood*, Hawthorn Press, Stroud

Nancy Mellon, *Storytelling with Children*, Hawthorn Press, Stroud

Rudolf Meyer, *The Wisdom of Fairy Tales*, Floris Books, Edinburgh

Lynne Oldfield, *Free to Learn*, Hawthorn Press, Stroud

— Crafts and activities

Joan Almon, *First Steps in Natural Dyeing*, Waldorf Kindergarten Assn of North America

Petra Berger, *Feltcraft*, Floris Books, Edinburgh

—, *The Christmas Craft Book*, Floris Books, Edinburgh

—, *Crafts Through the Year*, Floris Books, Edinburgh

Karin Neuschutz, *Creative Wool*, Floris Books, Edinburgh

Dagmar Schmidt and Freya Jaffke, *Magic Wool*, Floris Books, Edinburgh

Angelika Wolk-Gerche, *Creative Felt*, Floris Books, Edinburgh

—, *Making Fairy-tale Wool Animals*, Rudolf Steiner College Press, Fair Oaks

—, *More Magic Wool*, Floris Books, Edinburgh

Rotraud Reinhard, *A Felt Farm*, Floris Books, Edinburgh

Christine Schafer, *Magic Wool Fairies*, Floris Books Edinburgh

Magic Wool Kit, Floris Books, Edinburgh

— Story books, poetry and songs

Favourite Grimm's Tales, Floris Books, Edinburgh (includes Rumpelstiltskin and Mother Holle)

Reeve Lindbergh (ed.), *In Every Tiny Grain of Sand*, Walker Books, London

Brien Masters, *The Waldorf Song Book*, Floris Books, Edinburgh

Ann Pilling, *Before I go to sleep*, Kingfisher Books, London

Marlys Swinger (ed.), *Sing through the Day*, Plough Publishing House, New York & Sussex

Marlys Swinger (ed.), *Sing through the Seasons*, Plough Publishing House, New York & Sussex

Heather Thomas, *A Journey Through Time in Verse and Rhyme*, Floris Books, Edinburgh

Ineke Verschuren, *The Christmas Story Book*, Floris Books, Edinburgh

Craft suppliers

Australia:
Batik Oetoro
www.dyeman.com

Morning Star Crafts
www.morningstarcrafts.com.au

USA:
There are numerous sources of craft supplies in the USA, too many to list here. The Waldorf Early Childhood Association of North America maintains an excellent list on its website: www.waldorfearlychildhood.org/sources.asp

UK:
P&M Woolcraft
www.pmwoolcraft.co.uk

Fibrecrafts
www.fibrecrafts.com

Myriad Natural Toys
www.myriadonline.co.uk

Wild Colours
www.wildcolours.co.uk

Conservation of rare domestic animals

USA:
The American Livestock Breeds Conservancy
www.albc-usa.org

UK:
Rare Breeds Survival Trust
www.rbst.org.uk
The RBST website includes a list of Farm Parks to visit in the UK

Australia and New Zealand:
Rare Breeds Trust of Australia
www.rbta.org

Rare Breeds Conservation
Society of New Zealand
www.rarebreeds.co.nz

International:
SAVE Foundation
www.save-foundation.net/english/home.htm

The Children's Nature and Garden Centre

The Children's Nature and Garden Centre in Reichshof is open to all and offers seasonal nature classes. The Centre works closely with kindergartens and schools, and with parents. Its grounds are well equipped for practical, hands-on workshops, seminars and extended courses, and it also offers advice and support for those who want to set up similar schemes elsewhere.

For more information, contact the Centre at:

Natur-Kinder-Garten-Werkstatt Reichshof
Dorner Weg 4
51580 Reichshof
Germany

Tel: +49-22 61-52 22 1
Fax: +49-22 61-80 48 31
irmgardkutsch@aol.com

Photograph and Illustration Credits

Ingeborg Ludwig-Kersjes: p. 80 (I)
Gudrun Obermann: p. 10 (III)
Erika Salaw: p. 17 (I), 34 (I), 42, 84 (II)
Christian Tangemann: p. 30 (I), 32 (II), 35 (I), 72 (II), 74 (III, IV), 75 (II), 76 (I)
Anke Wilhelm: p. 10 (V, VI), 21, 22 (I, III), 24 (II), 26 (III, V, VI, VIII), 28 (I, II), 33 (I), 36 (I, III), 37, 39 (II), 45, 48 (I, III), 49, 54 (III), 56 (II, IV, VII, X), 59 (II), 65 (III), 69, 74 (II), 79 (I, II), 80 (III), 81 (I, II, IV), 84 (IV), 87 (I,II), 88 (I), 89 (I, II)
Wolpert & Strehle, Fotodesign (Stuttgart): 53 (I–III)

Edgar Bayer: p. 16, 37, 41–43, 45–47, 49, 73, 76, 77 (I,II)
Anke Wilhelm: p. 50, 51, 70, 71
Carolin Winkendick: p. 75
Many thanks to Theresa and all the children

All other photographs by Irmgard Kutsch

Nature Activities for All Seasons

SPRING
nature activities for children
Irmgard Kutsch & Brigitte Walden

SUMMER
nature activities for children
Irmgard Kutsch & Brigitte Walden

AUTUMN
nature activities for children
Irmgard Kutsch & Brigitte Walden

WINTER
nature activities for children
Irmgard Kutsch & Brigitte Walden